HOW TO CREATE THE PERFECT SALES WEBINAR

TABLE OF CONTENTS

FOREWORD

Webinars Saved My Life

Damn it!

As I pulled into the lot and parked outside my office window, I could see Donna, the HR Director loading my personal belongings into a box.

"No, you're not being fired," she lied through her teeth. "You're being laid off until business gets better".

13 years later and the phone still hasn't rung.

That's OK... In fact, it's FANTASTIC!

I didn't know it at the time. What I thought was one of the worst days of my life actually became the turning point that pivoted me into what I call "Second Act Success". I was able to create a new life for me and my family. One that gave me a great deal more money, more free time with the ones I love, and ultimately more security than a paycheck from a j.o.b. ever gave me.

And at the heart of my Second Act Success was a new skill I learned...

Webinars.

We live in magical times. From the palm of our hand, we can cast a massive net that spans the globe. At the very same time, we can focus with laser-like precision on a targeted audience that is eager to listen and learn from us.

Webinars allow us to take the stage or be the teacher at the front of the class. Our audience hears our voice and instantly knows, likes and trusts us. Simply by sharing your Passion, Experience and Talent (What I call "P.E.T." in my Second Act Success training) you can use webinars to gain customers that want to pay you for your knowledge.

Using this webinar strategy, I have built a worldwide audience of hundreds of thousands of people from 152 different countries.

And if I can do it, so can you.

But it has taken me nearly a decade to accomplish this. It took a lot of trial and error because there was never an instruction book for "How to Create the Perfect Sales Webinar" ...

Until NOW!

Yes, you now have in your hands the very instruction book that I wish I had years ago!

Not only that, but you are learning from somebody that I have come to know and respect as one of the true Masters of webinars, Mike Martin.

That praise does not come lightly. I have done hundreds of webinars with some of the biggest money makers. Mike Martin stands out at the very top of the list.

In fact, I met Mike on a webinar, and we became fast friends. Which proves my point about world-wide reach because Mike lives in the UK, and I live outside Dallas, Texas in the U.S.A...

So, take the time to study this book carefully. Keep it handy and return to it often. No matter what subject matter you want to monetize, Mike's tips, tricks and strategies will help you achieve your own "Second Act Success" a whole lot faster.

To Your Second Act Success,

Steve Rosenbaum

INTRODUCTION

THUMP THUMP, THUMP THUMP, THUMP THUMP, THUMP THUMP, the sound of my heart pounding against my chest echoed up into my temples.

My hands were clammy and shaking.

I had been to the toilet 5 or 6 times in the last 10 minutes.

I found myself checking the clock repeatedly, wishing I could freeze time for just a while. I did not feel ready for this.

I was scared. I was questioning my expertise. I was questioning everything I had told myself.

Was I making a mistake doing this Webinar? No, I told myself, but I am not sure I believed it at the time.

It was my first Webinar, and I had agreed to it at short notice, but as soon as I said yes, I also began to panic.

I spent the two weeks leading up to the Webinar nervous, grumpy, and petrified.

The night of the Webinar arrived, I sat in front of my computer, dreading the start of my speech.

The Webinar started, and the presenter began to introduce me as an expert. I felt out of my depth and nervous. Then he handed the microphone over to me.

My first words were, "Hello, welcome to the training. Can you please pop a one or a yes in the box to let me know you can hear me, OK? Also, can you please let me know that you can see my screen and what you are seeing?"

Within seconds I saw dozens of ones and yeses filling the screen. Prospects were writing what they saw on my screen and telling me they were looking forward to the training.

I had been petrified for over two weeks and questioned everything I was going to teach over and over, then suddenly, all the stress and all the worry drifted away.

My first Webinar went great, the audience reacted brilliantly to my training, and I made $16,000 in sales that very first night.

My Webinar was not perfect. It was far from perfect, but I still managed to have a great night, and I earned more money on that first night than I ever had before in a single day.

I do not care what business you are in, from selling cars to training students or even self-help. You can double your turnover with a webinar and skyrocket your company's success unbelievably.

If I lost everything today, I would find something to sell, and I would create a webinar to sell that product.

If I took a sales position at any company, I would make a webinar and use that Webinar to break all the sales records in that company by selling one to many.

There is no better or more cost-effective way of selling than creating your very own Webinar, and that is precisely what I am going to teach you to do inside this book.

I have been creating webinars for several years now, and I do them live at least three times a week. I regularly close 25 to 50% of the audience. However, I can close 90% of the audience when I focus on getting the right people into my presentation.

Everything in the book has been tried and tested in my webinars. I did not create all these techniques myself, some I did, and others I learned from books and friends along my journey.

I do not have a single webinar. I have many webinars and regularly write them for whatever I am selling on any given day.

Most presenters will have created one or two successful webinars in their life, and they have spent years honing them to perfection.

I spent months writing my very first Webinar and even longer improving it.

Without this book and the resources pack, it could easily take you 12 months to create a high-converting webinar, and you would need to do hundreds of hours of testing and spend thousands on ads to get it right.

You will save all that lost money and time because you have this book.

Be warned, creating your first Webinar will not be easy. You will need to commit yourself to this process, but once you have mastered this and have a high-converting webinar, you will never have to worry about money ever again.

This book is for two kinds of people, those who have something to sell and those who want to sell it using a live, like live or pre-recorded Webinar.

I did not write this book for you. I wrote this book for myself. So, I can download the "fill in the gaps slides" and use this book as a reference point every time I build a webinar.

If someone tells you they build webinars off the top of their head, I promise you they will miss out on crucial parts of their Webinar and lose sales.

You should print off the fill in the gaps documents every time you create a webinar and use this book as a reference manual.

I wish you all the luck in the World with your journey.

Let's get started!

Before taking another step, you should go to https://mikejmartin.com/webinar-resources/ and get your webinar resource pack to help you on your journey.

You will get:

- Fill in The Gaps Webinar Creation PDF
- Fill in The Gaps Webinar Slides PDF
- Fill in The Gaps Webinar Slides Google Drive Link (so you can download it into other formats)

EXPERT TIPS FOR YOUR WEBINAR

A WEBINAR SHOULD ONLY SOLVE ONE PROBLEM.

In the famous study, "Why Choice is Demotivating," Sheena Iyengar and Mark Lepper disputed the widespread belief that having more choice is a better sales strategy.

Several experiments found that people are more likely to buy products in a shop when offered fewer choices (6) instead of (24 or 30).

They even studied students and discovered that students were more likely to do an essay for extra credit when they were given a smaller list of six topics instead of 30 topics to choose from.

Those students who selected an essay from the smaller list of choices even wrote better quality essays.

Scientists call it "choice overload." In many product

categories, reducing the number of choices you offer a customer will improve the odds of making a sale. It might sound counter-intuitive, but it is best not to mess with how the human mind is wired. We are wired for simplicity and fewer choices. Do not try to change this. It will not work.

The biggest mistake I see people make when they create a webinar is that they are not quite sure who the Webinar is for, or even worse, they are creating a webinar for anyone. If you do not understand your audience, then you cannot sell to them.

A webinar should solve a specific problem for a particular audience. That way, you understand precisely who you are talking to and what problems they have in their business or life.

Let's look at a few headlines, so I can show you what I mean:

How to become a real estate millionaire without investing millions into property

This headline targets people wanting to get into real estate who do not have or do not want to risk millions of their capital.

Because we know the audience and understand what pushes their buttons, we can specifically cater our content to them.

Another good example could be:

6 Love tips to get any guy to fall head over heels in love with you.

This headline targets single women looking for love.

Again, we know the audience and understand what pushes their buttons so we can specifically cater our content to them.

Let's look at one final headline:

How to get 6 pack abs without going to the gym or changing what you eat

This headline is targeted at someone who wants a six-pack but does not want to work for it.

I have left this one until the end on purpose because it is obviously bullshit, but you would not believe how many people I have seen write a headline like this for their Webinar.

You can never live up to your claims if you talk absolute rubbish in your headline, and because of that, you may get an extremely high opt-in rate. However, you will convert very poorly because they are coming in with higher expectations than is possible, so no matter how good your offer is, it will never meet their expectations.

I would recommend finding a single problem your Webinar will solve and write all your content around solving that one problem.

Before going any further, think, what will your Webinar solve?

Just choose the problem. For now, you do not need to write a headline for your Webinar because we will cover that in more detail later.

You should answer these questions:

- What problem does your Webinar solve?
- What industry does the problem affect most?
- What sub-niche of this industry does the problem affect the most?
- Will they pay for the solution to the problem?
- Can they afford to pay for the solution to the problem?

You have your target audience, and this is who you should be talking to during your Webinar.

A WEBINAR SHOULD INSPIRE, NOT EDUCATE.

Peter is sitting in a bar with his friends from work complaining about his life.

An advert on the TV shows a 40 plus balding man with a potbelly just like Peter driving a bright red Ferrari down Los Angeles Boulevard.

Next to him is a hot blond-haired person at least 20 years younger than he is staring at him like she is madly in love with him.

As the man pulls into a swanky LA Hotel, all the other guests stop and stare at him like a movie star.

The man pulls up beside the valet, throws him the key, and disappears into the hotel with everyone enviously pointing and watching him.

The screen then fills with writing.

Is your life missing a brand-new Ferrari?

Peter goes out the very next day and gets in debt to buy himself a brand-new red Ferrari that will take him the next ten years to pay off.

He very soon realizes after purchase that:

- He can no longer help with the school run.
- He cannot afford to drive the car around town because it drinks fuel.
- He can barely get in and out of the car because his knees are going.
- The other families in the area laugh at him behind his back.
- He will have to cut corners in every other part of his life to afford this car.

He purchased the car on impulse because he got emotional and imagined his life would be so much better with that shiny new Ferrari.

Peter tells his friends he loves his car, he takes all the "you're a lucky bastard" comments from his mates down the pub, and he loves leaving his car keys on show for people to notice the Ferrari key that hangs from his keychain.

But there is not much else he likes about the car. In fact, he much preferred the economical seven-seater hybrid family car that he traded in for this one.

People buy on emotion and then later justify the purchase with logic. If the advert had not targeted his emotions, then Peter would have never purchased this vehicle.

Customers do not always immediately realize they need what you are selling them on your webinars. However, if you can make an emotional connection, they will justify the purchase logically later.

Unlike the Ferrari example, you should be selling customers something they need. Unfortunately, these powers can be used for evil, and many marketing agencies do just that.

My first Webinar focused mainly on emotion and did not answer many of the questions a future customer may have because I understood my Webinar was just an extended advertisement.

As time went by, I tried to improve my Webinar by adding more information, answering all the questions, and providing a more complete presentation.

I expected this to increase my sales, but it had the opposite effect. My Webinar got longer, and the information I provided improved, but the deals I made reduced massively.

I thought it was me and that I could not sell, that was until I asked a friend of mine to take a look at my Webinar.

He immediately said, you are teaching too much, not leaving enough out, and covering the subjects in too much detail.

"Your webinar should inspire, not educate," he said.

Teaching is for training courses and YouTube videos, not webinars. If you teach too much during your Webinar, you will kill your sales.

It is essential to understand that a webinar is an advertisement for your business, product, or service. Its only purpose is to get someone to act and purchase what you have to offer.

This will likely feel wrong when you are writing your Webinar, and I have no doubt you will want to teach all your best stuff, do not.

I am not saying you do not cover your best stuff. Just do not teach it in detail.

Imagine your Webinar helps businesses find new clients for their web design business. In summary, you might say something like this.

The complete process is:

- Go to the prospects' website on Google Chrome.
- Right-click and select "Inspect Element" or "Inspect."
- Click the "Lighthouse" tab
- Create Report & Save to Google Drive
- Open report template we give you.
- Add the share link to your report.
- Send the report to the business.
- Enjoy the rest of your day.

This is a recap from the end of a section from one of my webinars selling my product Magic Page Plugin to agencies, and as you can see, it provides all the steps in the process, but without the report, it is almost entirely useless.

It shows them how quick and easy they can complete this step which will get results, but if they want to get their hands on the report and everything else needed to achieve this, they must purchase.

The Webinar takes them through the steps they would follow on an average day and shares the results they will achieve when following these simple steps, but without what we have to offer at the end, it is just a numbered list.

This strategy may seem a little complicated at the minute. Do not worry. I will show you exactly how to piece all this together later in this book.

You should talk to the individual, not the audience.

I have an assistant who spends her days contacting high-value affiliates to see if they have the time to promote my webinars.

When she first started working for me, she had an opening email that went like this:

Hi NAME,

I saw your launch coming up on WHERE SHE SAW IT.

We took a look at your product, and I think we can help

you make additional sales from your launch.

If you have not already got a webinar on the back end of your launch, then we would love to talk to you about this.

I would love to arrange a conversation with you. Let me know if you are interested in discussing our Webinar that will pay you a 50% commission.

I look forward to hearing back from you soon.

Ta

Jen

As you can imagine, this did not convert very well, and we hardly got any responses when sending this message to potential prospects.

She tried several different messages over a period and finally settled on this:

Hi, name.

My manager passed me your name and asked me to contact you directly because he said you are respected in the industry, and he would love to work with you.

We currently have 3 100% automated webinars that all convert at $20+ EPC from just a simple email.

If you are looking for something solid to mail, I would love to share our webinars with you.

Please let me know if this would be, OK?

This message skyrocketed the number of responses we got and increased the number of promotions we receive from 3rd parties massively.

At first, we were getting about 1 in 50 responses to our messages, and now we get about 2 in 10, which might not sound remarkable. Still, when those individuals can be worth $10,000 each repeat income to the business, it is a very cost-effective marketing strategy. All we did to improve the message was speak to them personally rather than talk about what they are doing.

Nobody likes to be ignored or feel like they are just another face in the crowd. People love it when a company or person addresses them personally and compliments them. That is why this is so powerful.

Many of the World's best speakers have a way of making you feel like they are talking directly to you and make you feel like you are both part of the same team.

They do not do this by accident. It is intentional because they know it results in you agreeing with the narrative and acting the way they want.

It can be OK to talk to the audience when presenting to a large room of people. However, a webinar is quite different, and on a sales webinar, it is rarely OK.

To the prospect, there is you speaking and them listening, sitting in a room, usually on their own with their computer.

If you address the individual rather than addressing the room, it will feel more personal, and they will feel like you are speaking directly to them.

This way of speaking increases the feeling that you are talking directly to the individual and makes them feel like you have answered all their questions directly.

As a result of this, you will find that sales increase.

This is a straightforward thing to do. After you have finished writing your Webinar, go through and look for anywhere you address the entire audience and change it.

For example, you may ask can anyone answer this question? Or does anyone know the answer to this? In situations like this, simply change it to do you know the answer to this? or can you answer this?

It is quite simple and very powerful. It will make the attendees feel like you are speaking to them directly and increase engagement because they feel like you are calling them directly to action.

LOOPS WILL KEEP YOUR CUSTOMERS ON TO THE END.

What is a loop? A loop is a statement designed to make your audience want to remain on the presentation to find out the answer, receive a gift or benefit.

I have tested doing this in many ways. Some have failed, and some have worked. The ones that worked best include prize draws, free access to an otherwise premium product, and educational content.

You can add many of these throughout the presentation, and as you get better at delivering presentations, you will be able to open multiple loops, closing them gradually.

The best speakers will open a loop, then open another before closing the first one, then open the third loop before closing the second, and so on.

When first practicing this technique, I recommend

concentrating on opening a single loop early in the presentation that hooks the listener to the end.

A standard webinar timeline will look like this:

A webinar timeline with loops will look like this:

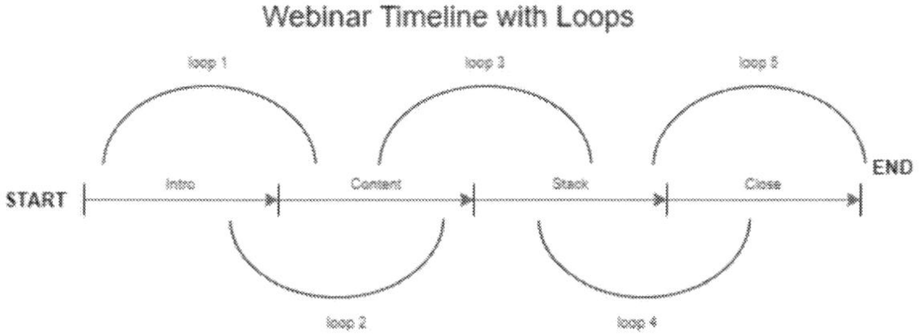

As you can see, a second loop starts before the previous one is closed. You will see loops like this all the time but not realize it.

Weekly TV Shows will close on a loop to make sure you tune in the following week, and films will also do the same. One of the most famous ones was Luke Skywalker's Dad in the Star Wars franchise.

When watching TV, you should look for these, and you will spot them everywhere.

Here is an example; I have a presentation for people looking to learn Rank & Rent (it is Webinar three on this page if you want to watch it https://www.mikejmartin.com/webinars/) And in that presentation, I list the three things they will learn today (the three sections of my presentation).

I then go on to state; If you stay until the end, I will show you:

"How you can use the 80/20 principle and two simple questions to rent out your websites for a high monthly fee."

For the wrong audience, this is crap, and they have no reason to stay on the presentation, but for the right audience who have been struggling for months or even years to rent out their websites, this is something they want the answer to, and because of that they will stay until the end.

If every person your message connects with remains on until the end, then there is a good chance they will buy.

It is easy to keep the wrong audience on by saying we will give you an iPad or we will give you access to software for free, but the best way to hook someone to the end is with something that relates to what you are offering, in this case, something that helps their business.

The number of people on the Webinar at the end may not be as high with this approach, but they will be the people interested in your offer.

THE MORE YOUR AUDIENCE NODS THEIR HEAD, THE MORE YOU WILL SELL.

Have you ever found yourself watching a presentation or listening to a speech and nodding along as they speak?

When something finally clicks with you and makes sense, you involuntarily nod your head in agreement?

Are you doing it right now?

Did you just do it again?

Powerful, isn't it? And it is such a simple thing to do that you can weave it into the way you speak in your presentation.

If you can get the audience nodding their head every couple of minutes throughout your presentation, your conversions will skyrocket.

There are many straightforward ways to do this when you first get started, and as you get better at writing webinars, you will find ways to include these micro-commitments right into the way you speak rather than simply asking questions. Does that make sense?

Did you just nod again? :)

This is such a simple technique that many presenters forget to do it, but this can be used in presentations, in sales letters, in conversations, in fact, in anything you do.

I find myself using these micro-commitments with my kids, my partner, and even my friends. I have gotten so used to doing it that it is just how I speak now.

Some of the more common ways to get a nod are as follows:

- Am I right?
- Do you agree?
- Does that make sense?
- Is this making sense?
- Can you see how that works?
- Has this ever happened to you?
- Would you do it like that?
- I am sure you can see how this works.
- Do you understand?
- Are you ready for this?
- Do you want this?

There are hundreds of these, and they work because each time your audience nods their head, it is a micro-commitment they agree with you.

Big companies use this when they are collecting information in forms. You will notice all the yes and no or multiple choice select questions are at the start of the forms on their websites.

They also split the form into sections. You add just one piece of information and click next.

This is them getting lots of micro-commitments from you before asking for your personal information like email, address, name, and phone number.

This technique can improve form submissions by 300%. Imagine what it could do for your sales.

It would help if you practiced this technique daily with your partner, your children, at work, and even during your daily life with the public. You should notice things start going your way a lot easier without any additional effort, and eventually, you will without even trying.

QUESTIONS = ENGAGEMENT = ACTION

This might seem obvious after reading the chapter, "The more your audience nods their head, the more you will sell." Presenters tend to talk at the audience and not involve them.

As you can see from the chapter above, "The more your audience nods their head, the more you will sell" we use questions to get the audience to nod their heads. However, there are many other ways we can use questions to keep the audience engaged.

Questionnaires are a brilliant way to engage the audience or prizes for solving a problem. For example, at the start of an important part of your presentation, you could say.

"I want you to listen carefully during this section because I'm going to ask you about this in a few minutes and the first person with the right answer gets STATE PRIZE."

This means everyone is listening when you need

them to, and the answers you want them to learn sink in. These answers should be something that reinforces your messages and helps knock down objections they may have about buying your offer at the end of the Webinar.

A fantastic tool for this is Google forms, you can share a link during a presentation to a questionnaire or quiz, and as they complete the form, you receive the answers live and can confirm who got the highest score.

I like to read out each question, confirm the answer, then reveal who got the highest score at the end. This is good for getting the audience to learn the correct answers, and those answers can then be weaved into the offer.

You can also simply use questions to get the audience involved. "Can you answer this? Please answer in the chat, or can you tell me this?" These types of questions work brilliantly.

Whatever method suits your style best, I would suggest using questions and engagement techniques throughout your presentation to avoid sending your audience to sleep.

PEOPLE BUY FROM PEOPLE THEY LIKE, AND THEY LIKE PEOPLE WHO ARE LIKE THEM OR WHO THEY ASPIRE TO BE LIKE

Remember earlier when I said you need to know your audience and understand who you are selling to?

This is one of those times when knowing your audience is crucial, and when used correctly, it can be very powerful indeed.

This section's problem is that presenters tend to misuse it and come across as show-offs instead of becoming someone the audience wants to be like.

They show huge houses and flash cars, which they have hired or photoshopped for the presentation in most cases, and they talk about how much money they earn and how easy their lives are.

You are not looking to make the audience jealous of you but instead, make them see that you are successful now (how they aspire to be) and come from a similar position to where they are now (you are like them).

This covers both angles and is relatively easy to achieve without showing off.

Stories can help the audience connect with you, and they can also enable you to drop subtle hints that both show you are successful and that you started from a similar place to where they are right now.

You could tell a simple story of how you still drive your old white transit van you had when you were on the road working hard for a living and that it is nice to drive the Bentley you bought for your other half now and again, but the van reminds you of where you came from, and you intend to use it until it dies.

Or explain how when you bought your mother a four-bedroom detached bungalow for Christmas, she was so surprised because a card and a box of chocolates were all you could afford in previous years.

You do not want to copy these stories. You should use your own true stories to show the audience you are successful and started from a similar place to where they are right now.

This helps build rapport with your audience and shows that what you do works.

People buy from people they like, and they like people who are like them or who are like they aspire to be.

SELL THE OUTCOME, NOT THE PRODUCT.

I am sitting in my front room watching morning TV when a man comes on asking if I want to win £100,000.

He then explains just how easy it is, reads out the phone number twice before instructing me to ring the number on the screen right now.

He tells me to imagine holding the money in my hand and imagine what I would do with the money.

He then asks would you pay off your mortgage? Would you buy a brand-new car? Or would you take the whole family on holiday?

You could even do all three. It is a substantial life-changing amount of money, and it could be yours.

Just pick up the phone right now and call the number on this screen.

Can you see what he is doing? He is selling me the outcome. He is making me picture having £100,000 and making me think about how great my life could be with that money.

This strategy works amazingly well and increases the number of people picking up the phone and calling tenfold.

I also see them do something similar most days with flash cars or big houses, and every single time they sell me the pleasure that winning will bring.

If they just showed £100,000 on the screen and said win this or showed a Range Rover and said win this, the number of calls would reduce massively.

This is one of the biggest mistakes I see presenters make when they are creating a presentation. Let me show you an example.

If I was selling my lead automation tool Lead Simplify, I might say:

Lead Simplify is the World's first system publicly available that enables you to build an unlimited number of web forms that can be added to any website anywhere in the World.

The forms collect leads, bring them into your system, sort them, and sell them to your lead buyers for you.

The system can also manage your phone numbers so that a caller can ring up and input their zip code and choose an industry. They get redirected to the right lead buyer in the right location and the right sector.

You can collect unlimited leads by phone and form and

use Lead Simplify to process them all.

We also have a built-in invoicing system that you can use for pre and post-pay clients to put them on a contract or have them use pay as they go.

This system has so many features it will revolutionize your business and bring it into the 21st century.

Are you falling asleep yet?

I could go on for hours like this and send everyone in the room to sleep.

This is what I see too many presenters do, they send their audience to sleep with all the bullshit, but if you have the right people in the room from the start, you do not need to talk crap. You can sell the outcome and involve them in the process.

If I have the correct headline and I have the right people on the Webinar, then I would say:

Do you have a team answering your phones?

Answer: YES

Do you have a sales team?

Answer: YES

Do you have a lead buyer onboarding team?

Answer: YES

Do you have an accounts team sorting all your invoices and chasing payments?

Answer: YES

Does this cost you a fortune?

Answer: YES

If you could replace most of this team with a single piece of software that only costs $97 a month, would that be amazing?

Answer: YES

SOLD

I have not bored the crap out of the audience and sent them all to sleep. Instead, I have involved them, and I have let them answer all the questions with lots of little micro-commitments.

They are involved, they understand precisely what the product does, and I have shown the product's value and proved it would save them money, so the cost is irrelevant.

Does that make sense?

The above script used a lot of micro-commitments which had the audience nodding the whole time.

If I had a room full of Ice Cream Salesmen in the Webinar, this would not have worked. That is why it is essential to know who you are selling to and have the right audience on the Webinar.

PEOPLE WANT WHAT THEY CANNOT HAVE.

Have you ever heard the saying that the grass is not greener on the other side?

It is in our nature to look at other people's lives, businesses, assets, homes, even partners and think they have it better than we do.

The truth is they usually do not, but we believe they do because it is Human nature to want what we cannot have.

We can easily take advantage of this during our Webinar.

We limit the number of special offers we have available. If you have 50 people in a room and know your webinar converts at 20%, you will make ten sales.

If you limit this to the first 12, then the usual 10 will buy, and then you can explain we have two left, and the price will increase back to 10 times this deal price once they are gone.

This will usually push another two people in your audience to jump on board and take advantage of the offer. If you do three webinars a week, this is six sales a week and over 300 more customers a year, not bad for something that takes less than a minute to implement into your Webinar.

Most webinar presenters will not limit the number of sales to what they say. Other people on the Webinar cannot see how many people buy, so they use this as purely a means of making more sales.

They count down. We now only have three remaining. Now there are two. OK, we are on the last one before this offer is gone forever. They could be making tens of sales on each number, but the audience is none the wiser.

QVC are experts in this, and they run their sales 24 hours a day, and on every product, there is always a limit and a countdown timer for when the offer will close. We will discuss the countdown timer shortly.

IF THEY DO NOT BUY ON THE DAY, THEY WILL LIKELY NEVER BUY.

After generating millions from running hundreds of webinars, presentations, and talks, I can confidently say that the audience will usually not buy if they do not buy the first time they watch the presentation.

This is more so when you are presenting to cold traffic from Ads. Some affiliates may have a relationship with their audience where very few people show up live because they know there will be a replay, and they buy then, however in most cases, customers who do not buy live will not buy.

If they have seen the presentation once, they are unlikely to watch the entire presentation again and go all the way through and buy your offer.

This is not to say you should not run the replay to the audience because you will still make sales from the replays to people who did not show up live and therefore have not already seen the Webinar.

Do not confuse a replay to attendees with a replay to non-attendees because those who do not show up on the live will be watching the Webinar for the first time.

Taking this into account, you need to get as many people as possible to purchase your offer, service, or product the very first time they watch your presentation.

A fantastic way to do this is by adding a countdown timer at the end of your presentation. I do not do anything fancy with this, and I do not try to superimpose a countdown timer on the screen. I just add a 5-minute video to the end of my webinars.

I will say something like, OK, we are running out of time. You have just 5 minutes to take advantage of this offer, and then it has gone forever.

I will share a 5-minute countdown video while I try to answer all your questions in the chat.

We have hundreds of people on live today. I will try to answer all your questions. Please add three question marks to the start of your questions so I can spot them.

If we miss your question, do not worry. You can jump on board today and submit your questions to support@mysupporturl.com, and my team will look after you.

Remember, we have a 30 day no questions asked

money-back guarantee, so if you jump on board today and it is not for you, then it costs you nothing to test this fantastic deal, and you can even keep the gifts.

You cannot usually take the gifts back anyway, so using this to push them over the line can be just the push they need to make the decision.

PEOPLE DO NOT GIVE A SHIT ABOUT YOU.

When writing your Webinar, you may fall into the trap of talking more about yourself than explaining how your service will help them. If you talk about you, make sure it is to help them see themselves in your shoes.

It is easy to ramble on for hours about what you and your clients have done, but it is also easy to forget that most clients could not care less about you or your other clients, so keep this short.

If you have written a great headline and have the right kind of people on your Webinar, you have a good idea about what they do for a living or what they are interested in doing.

This knowledge enables you to steer the content and show how your product can help them rather than explaining how you or existing clients have used it already.

Potential customers are looking for a reason to say

this will not work for me, and if you give them that, you will lose them entirely and never get them onto one of your presentations ever again.

I used to be a locksmith, and most of what I did started from growing an extensive network of lead generation websites in the locksmith industry.

Because of this, I used to show a lot of examples from my own business. I noticed that one of the most frequent questions I used to get on a webinar was "I'm in plumbing, will this work for me?" or roofing or "I deal with divorce lawyers will this work for me?"

I got tired of saying yes, this will work for any industry, so I created a slide that said:

Do not worry if you are looking at this and thinking, well, I am not a locksmith. Will this work for me? Because this works for any industry that has local search online. When you think about it, that is almost every industry because most industries are searched at a local or city level online.

After adding this into my presentation, it got rid of that question and increased sales because no one is left asking themselves if this will work for them because they know it will.

It is very easy to talk about your business, but you must remember to let the listeners know it also fits into their industry. If it does not work for them, let them know, and there is a chance they will attend your future presentations because you have not wasted their time.

If you make them wait until the end to find out it does not work for them, then they will never attend a webinar you are hosting ever again.

So, remember, customers like to know what is in it for them, and the sooner you can let them know this, the more they will pay attention to the rest of your presentation.

THERE IS ABSOLUTELY NO RISK TO YOU.

If you have the right offer, and your product or service does what you say it does, then you can confidently give a money-back guarantee.

Do not forget we concentrated on getting the right audience into the room, we hooked them to the end, and they are now listening to your offer, but they may be a little unsure if it fits what they need.

Adding a 30-day no-questions-asked money-back guarantee to the end of the offer and stating you can try this at completely no risk to you for the next 29 days will skyrocket the number of sales you make.

If you are selling a decent product or service and your offer does exactly what you say it will, then your refund rate will remain incredibly low, and the number of sales you make will massively increase.

Also, in certain countries, you have to offer a certain refund period by law. The buyers may not even know about the refund period you have to provide.

Therefore, stating it as a no-questions-asked refund puts a positive spin on local legislation you must adhere to anyway.

YOU ARE NOT A ROBOT, SO DO NOT ACT LIKE ONE.

Failure to listen here will destroy your sales and have people running for the hills if they hear you are the speaker at an event, on a webinar, or at a presentation.

We have all sat in a room, on a presentation, at a wedding or funeral, and thought to ourselves, is this person ever going to shut up?

The speech might not be excessively long, but it feels like it is lasting a lifetime, and you do not know why just that the speaker is sending you to sleep with every word that comes out of their mouth.

This type of snooze fest usually happens when the speaker is using their so-called radio or presenter voice.

Unless they are a brilliant actor, this causes the presenter to speak in a very monotone way without any emotion or pitch changes.

What is happening here is the person is trying to sound professional and pronounce all their words correctly, but in doing so, they are sending the audience to sleep.

If you have an accent, embrace it. If you speak fast, then speak fast. If you are always excited, then be excited. The audience will sense your emotion, and your voice will change regularly from low pitch to high pitch and everything in the middle.

Unbelievably, this is one of the most important parts of your Webinar because the audience cannot always see your face, and they can very rarely see your body language. The only thing they have to judge your sincerity is your voice, and trust me, if this is not sincere, the audience will know.

I have read in so many books that you need to pronounce your words correctly and that you need to speak slowly and steadily so everyone can understand you, but trust me, nothing could be further from the truth when you are trying to sell from the stage or on a webinar.

Watch speakers like Grant Cardone, Russell Brunson, or Jason Fladlien. You will see that neither of these speak perfectly, none of them speak monotone, and none of them avoid MMMs and ERRs because they are human, and they talk like you and I do when we talk to our family or friends, just with a little more excitement.

When speaking on a webinar, you want to be yourself, and you want to be honest and natural, or the audience will sense you are not sincere, and your sales will suffer.

If you struggle to get excited about what you are selling, or you hate selling it, then you are selling the wrong thing for you. You will notice all successful speakers who sell from stage or on webinars believe in what they are selling, and that shows through in their voice.

FACTS TELL - STORIES SELL

A few months back we decided to buy a new TV because the one we had was several years old and there was a very thin red line running from the top to the bottom of the screen that you could not help but stare at when watching TV.

We went to the local department store and walked around looking at TVs, commenting on how lifelike specific pictures were and how grainy others were.

When the salesperson eventually came over and asked if he could help us, I asked what the best TV you have with the best picture is. He pointed me in the direction of the TV that had its own section of the shop and a price tag to match.

I looked at Lorna and asked, "you want that one?" she smiled back at me, and I intuitively knew that was the TV for us.

Now let us fast forward a few months. We have this fantastic television we love, and feel was worth every penny we paid for it.

We spend about an hour together every morning

watching TV after we drop the kids at school, and we discuss all the things going on in our lives at the minute.

This one morning last week, Lorna jumped up from the sofa and erupted into a rage. Scratches and fingerprints were all over the bottom left corner of the TV, where our baby girl had dug her nails into the screen.

Lorna, almost in tears, looked at me and said, "she's ruined the TV."

I knew exactly how the scratches had happened and exactly how the baby had done them, so I began to explain.

"Lorna, you know when I sit with Alexis every morning and watch GMB while she wakes up slowly before nursery?"

"YES," she responds, still a little angry.

"Well, the other morning, I was watching Good Morning Britain on ITV, and they have this little logo in the bottom left corner of the TV."

"It rotates between ITV and GMB initials and kind of turns over and has a 3D effect while the news is playing."

"OK," she replied.

"The other morning, I went into the kitchen to make a cup of coffee, and I left the news on while Alexis was in the living room. When I returned, she was standing in front of the TV trying to grab the logo from the screen."

Lorna's face changed from anger to a loving smile instantly as she pictured our little girl innocently trying to pluck the logo from inside the TV.

Whenever we see that rotating logo on the bottom left corner of the TV or spot those annoying little scratches, we are filled with a loving memory of our little girl trying to pluck the logo from the TV.

Can you see how easily a small story can instantly change the way someone feels about something forever and just how powerful the right story at the right time can be?

There is a saying you will hear a lot in sales; Facts tell, but stories sell. This saying means if you want to sell to somebody, then you need to tell them a story.

This saying does not mean you cannot sell with facts, but if you need to use facts, then you will do a lot better if you weave them into a story.

Sales is all about building a rapport with the customer as quickly as possible while also helping them see themselves benefiting from what you have to offer.

A great place to start when telling a story for your Webinar is implementing a basic structure and then adding or subtracting where needed.

My story structure is as follows:

- I wanted to achieve this.
- I tried by doing this.

- I failed.
- I thought all hope was lost until I discovered this.
- I changed how I did it and started doing it like this instead.
- I achieved success.

I like to use this structure to explain how I wanted to achieve something my audience wants.

I then explain how I tried doing it the same way they are trying to do it or how they are being told to do it by the so-called experts.

Next, I reveal how doing it this way did not give me the results I expected, and I either failed or got very poor results following the so-called status quo.

I then elaborate on the hopelessness I felt when I realized this was not going to work and that I needed to start from nothing if I wanted to achieve what I had set out to achieve.

Then comes the turning point in the story, when I suddenly realize why it is never worked the old way and how the new way of doing it is so much better.

This strategy is usually something I learn from a 3rd party or from watching and learning from someone else. Donald Miller refers to this person as the guide in "Building A Story Brand" (I recommend reading this).

I then explain how I completely changed the way I approach the problem. I tackle the problem the new way, and it has enabled me to achieve easily what my audience is struggling to achieve the old way.

If you take the listener on a journey with you via your story, they will hopefully have the exact AHA moment you had. They will completely understand why the old way does not work, and you end up with a customer for life.

Let me share a snippet from one of my webinars that illustrates my story structure for you:

When I first discovered Rank & Rent, I was going to take over the World *(I WANTED TO ACHIEVE THIS)*

I thought I could easily, Build, Rank and Rent Websites in hundreds of industries.

I started with 5 *(I TRIED BY DOING THIS)*

Plumbers, Roofers, Electricians, Locksmiths and Pest Control

I decided I was going to target all these industries myself and completely crush it.

I set out on my journey and started building websites in all these industries.

I was researching all these industries.

I was writing content in all these industries.

I was building backlinks in all these industries.

And before I knew it

I had become a busy fool *(I FAILED)*

My days were filled with busy.

My head was filled with clutter.

But my bank wasn't filled with money.

I discussed my dilemma with my mother, who was still alive at the time.

And she just smiled and said, "One step at a time Michael."

Confused, I asked what she meant.

"What happens if we focus on too much?" she asked.

"I don't know?" I asked, still confused.

"You can't give anything your full attention, so nothing gets done right. Pick an industry and take that first," she answered. (MY GUIDE)

I had heard this so many times about focus, people saying multitasking destroys productivity and focus. But I never realized I was multitasking until my mother pointed it out.

She was right I was jumping from one thing to another and never giving anything my full attention.

I listened for the first time in my life.

I decided to take locksmiths.

All my efforts went into building locksmith websites (I CHANGED HOW I DID IT AND I STARTED DOING IT LIKE THIS INSTEAD)

All my studying was based around locksmiths and their websites.

I looked at terminology.

I looked at how people searched online for locksmiths.

I even looked at how backlinks were built to their websites and how many links they had on average.

And within a few months, I had dozens of websites built and ranking.

Some were rented out, and from some, I sold the leads.

I became well known in the locksmith industry as a specialist for locksmith websites.

And within 12 months, I had over 200 businesses renting my websites or paying me for leads every single month *(I ACHIEVED SUCCESS)*

So, let me ask you.

What is the number one rule you must follow when building your own Rank & Rent Business?

The Golden Rule - Choose a niche and become a specialist in that niche *(THEY NOW UNDERSTAND WHY THIS WAY WORKS AND THE OLD WAY DOESN'T)*

If you can structure the key points, you want your audience to understand like this, you will have customers who understand your strategy at a much higher level, and they will adopt your strategy and thank you for their success.

If you watch Webinar 3 from this page https://www.mikejmartin.com/webinars/ you will see I throw an additional spanner in the works at the end of this story that moves them on to part three of the presentation.

The most important thing you will learn from this book is how to structure your stories right so that they do the selling for you.

I usually try to add three stories into a presentation, and each one leads on from the last and enhances my message throughout the content section. However, that is not where the power of these stories end.

If I need to help them understand something else in my presentation, then I also use a story and loosely follow this structure. Whenever I am selling anything, I will use this story structure if possible.

HOW TO STRUCTURE YOUR WEBINAR

A webinar has five main sections or building blocks, and getting any of them wrong can cause the entire Webinar to fail.

Many presenters concentrate on the content section and then add the other parts of the Webinar after it is finished. Focusing mainly on the content section can result in them rushing the other sections of the Webinar, which will negatively affect their results even if their content section is amazing.

The sections of a webinar are:

- The Title
- The Introduction
- The Content
- The Irresistible Offer
- The Questions & Answers

I will go through these in order in this book, but you can create them in any order you prefer. If you know what your content section will be, then make it first.

If you feel like you have a fantastic introduction but are unsure of the content or the offer sections, make that section first.

Remember, all sections are created separately and given your total care and attention when making them. Do not rush any part of your Webinar, or you may miss something crucial and end up with a dud.

The great news is that if your Webinar is created this way, then even a dud can be saved by tracking drop-off and fixing the failing part of your Webinar.

THE TITLE

The title is the most overlooked part of any webinar. I have read every book I can find on webinars, and most of them do not even mention the webinar title.

If you have a terrible title, nobody will see your Webinar. If you have a great title that does not target your audience correctly, many of the wrong people will see your Webinar.

I see many ad companies who only concentrate on cost per opt-in, but in most cases, this results in you getting the wrong people into your Webinar.

They use this to show they are doing their job correctly, but as a result, it destroys your Webinar because the wrong people are watching.

The key to a good title is to target the correct audience specifically and include some curiosity so they will not look and think, "***I know what that is about,***" and not show up!

Titles should fulfill three things:

- They target a specific audience.
- They provide something the specific audience wants to achieve without the pain it would usually take.

- They have curiosity.

My favorite kind of webinar titles will be structured something like this.

How to _SOMETHING THEY WANT_ without _PAIN THEY DON'T WANT_

NUMBER ways to _SOMETHING THEY WANT_ without _PAIN THEY DON'T WANT_

Let me give you an example:

10 ways to get more sales without increasing your ad budget.

This title covers pleasure without pain, and it has the curiosity to get a tremendous show-up rate. However, it does not target a specific audience, so the wrong people will attend and leave early feeling disappointed.

10 ways to get more sales on Amazon without increasing your ad budget.

This title has curiosity because it does not tell the audience how. It says they will not need to increase their spending, and it targets people selling on Amazon.

If you can satisfy all three elements when creating your webinar title, you will get a great show-up rate from the audience you want to see your presentation.

THE INTRODUCTION

When creating an introduction to your Webinar, do not concentrate on time or how long this section will be because I have seen this on many webinars, and the presenter ends up talking for talking sake. They end up pissing the audience off or just boring them to death.

I made this mistake myself when I first started creating webinars. I followed all the rules, and I could see when I downloaded the chat that people were getting pissed off because I was filling the time as I had been told to, and it was just irritating.

An introduction must cover a few things but do not ramble on. Remember, the audience is there to watch your content section, so once the introduction has fulfilled its purpose, move on.

Your introduction should let the audience know:

- Why they should listen to you (achievements or what makes you great)
- What you have done for others (other achievements through you or client suc-

cess)

- What their future will look like after this (something they want but until now have failed to achieve)
- The challenges they will face (what is hard about what your teaching)
- What they should expect from the presentation (who this is for and what you will cover)
- Why they should stay until the (give them a reason to stay until the end)

That is it. If you can cover these 6 points in under 5 minutes and get your point across, that is completely fine. If it takes 20 minutes and is all relevant, and you are not just rambling on, that is OK.

I used to follow the 90-minute rule with my webinars because everyone in the industry said you must stay on as long as possible, and it will increase sales because they have committed more time to your presentation.

I listened at first, but then I started to ask a question every time someone told me my Webinar needed to be longer.

Have you ever done a webinar that is under 90 minutes? I would ask.

Most of the people offering this advice had never done a webinar under the 90-minute mark. They had just listened to what the market was saying, and they followed suit.

I decided to do the testing and see if the 90-minute to 2-hour time was better than a shorter webinar of under an hour. Guess what it made absolutely no difference to the number of sales I made when I compared the number of attendees still on the Webinar to the total number of sales.

In fact, there was less drop-off with the shorter webinars, so there were more people still on when I started my pitch, which increased how many sales I made overall.

It also meant I was not filling the Webinar with crappy content just to make up the time, like this book.

This is a short book because I have added exactly what you need to know, and there is completely no fluff. Isn't that better than a 700-page book that provides the same advice plus 500 pages of rambling?

Anyway, when creating an introduction, I would recommend making it as long as it needs to be to get the message across and no longer.

Simply copy and paste the list above into a PowerPoint presentation and answer the six questions so the audience understands the answer to each point. (Do not leave the questions on the slides, just use them as prompts for your content)

THE CONTENT

Remember when I said earlier, your Webinar should have a single point of belief that your message is built around, and you should emphasize that message repeatedly during the Webinar.

The whole presentation is designed to help the audience believe just one thing, and it is the job of your content section to make them believe that one thing before you make your offer.

The content section has three main goals, so you should break them down into three sections. Each section will take the listener one step closer to believing what you have to offer will change their life for the better.

The three sections can be broken down as follows:

- Section one - prove what you are offering works.
- Section two - prove that they have the ability to do this.
- Section three - prove that there are no outside forces that can stop them.

When trying to help an audience member believe something, I like to use stories because stories tend to stick, and people remember them.

I have a structure I try to use with all my stories, which presses all the right buttons and motivates the listeners to act.

My story structure is as follows:

- I wanted to achieve this.
- I tried by doing this.
- I failed.
- I thought all hope was lost until I discovered this.
- I changed how I did it and started doing it like this instead.
- I achieved success.

Let me share a brief story I use in one of my presentations to show you what I mean.

I wanted the audience who were building a rank and rent business from scratch to believe that the only way to scale a rank and rent business is to choose a niche and become a specialist in that niche.

This is true, but if I tell them that they will not listen, I go back to when I first discovered this and tell them the story.

My story, which you may remember from earlier, goes a little something like this:

When I first discovered Rank & Rent, I was going to take over the World.

I thought I could easily, Build, Rank and Rent Out Web-

sites in hundreds of industries.

I started with 5.

Plumbers, Roofers, Electricians, Locksmiths and Pest Control

I decided I was going to target all these industries myself and completely crush it.

I set out on my journey and started building websites in all these industries.

I was researching all these industries.

I was writing content in all these industries.

I was building backlinks in all these industries.

And before I knew it

I had become a busy fool.

My days were filled with busy.

My head was filled with clutter.

But my bank wasn't filled with money.

I discussed my dilemma with my mother, who was still alive at the time.

And she just smiled and said, "One step at a time Michael."

Confused, I asked what she meant.
"What happens if we focus on too much?" she asked.

"I don't know?" I asked, still confused.

"You can't give anything your full attention, so nothing gets done right. Pick an industry and take that

first," she answered.

I had heard this so many times about focus, people saying multitasking destroys productivity and focus. But I never realized I was multitasking until my mother pointed it out.

She was right I was jumping from one thing to another and never giving anything my full attention.

I listened for the first time in my life.

I decided to take locksmiths.

All my efforts went into building locksmith websites.

All my studying was based around locksmiths and their websites.

I looked at terminology.

I looked at how people searched online for locksmiths.

I even looked at how backlinks were built to their websites and how many links they had on average.

And within a few months, I had dozens of websites built and ranking.

Some were rented out, and from some, I sold the leads.

I became well known in the locksmith industry as a specialist for locksmith websites.

And within 12 months, I had over 200 businesses renting my websites or paying me for leads every single month

So, let me ask you.

What is the number one rule you must follow when

building your own Rank & Rent Business?

The Golden Rule - Choose a niche and become a specialist in that niche.

Can you see how this story takes them from not understanding why they need to choose a niche and become specialists in that niche right to understanding and believing in the concept?

They now know why they need to do this. They can see the pitfalls of not doing this, and they will not forget this story, so it will remain with them throughout their life and will always help them.

For each of the three sections of your webinar content, you should create a story like this one.

You should break your content into three sections and follow this framework:

Section one - prove what you are offering works.

- Create a section title: How to ________ without ____________
- Tell a story that follows:
    - I wanted to achieve this.
    - I tried by doing this.
    - I failed.
    - I thought all hope was lost until I discovered this.
    - I changed how I did it and started doing it like this.
    - I achieved this.
- Share some social proof.

Section two - prove that they have the ability to do this.

- Create a section title: How to ________ without ___________
- Tell a story that follows:
  - I wanted to achieve this.
  - I tried by doing this.
  - I failed.
  - I thought all hope was lost until I discovered this.
  - I changed how I did it and started doing it like this.
  - I achieved this.
- Share some social proof.

Section three - prove that there are no outside forces that can stop them.

- Create a section title: How to ________ without ___________
- Tell a story that follows:
  - I wanted to achieve this.
  - I tried by doing this.
  - I failed.
  - I thought all hope was lost until I discovered this.
  - I changed how I did it and started doing it like this.
  - I achieved this.
- Share some social proof.

Let me explain in a little more detail how each section of your content works.

For section one:

I like to share some knowledge and explain how I gained that knowledge, as with the story above.

For section two:

I like to share what makes our strategy work so much better than the competition.

You should make your offer into a new opportunity, do not just improve on what others already offer in your industry, or they have no reason to move.

With the Webinar above in section two, I explain how they can stick a pin in a map and draw a big circle around it for every single area the business wants to work. (Its Webinar 3 on this page if you're going to watch it https://www.mikejmartin.com/webinars/)

I then show them how they can use Magic Page Plugin (the tool we are selling) to make just one extra page for their website that will automatically build almost SEO perfect web pages for every single area.

This strategy will 10x the number of leads they are getting from their website with a single piece of content.

If they can create a single piece of content and they can, then they can do this, but it is only possible with our software.

For section three:

I like to share another little golden nugget that will blow their mind to the point of wanting to jump on right away.

We will show them that even if they are fighting a battle against some big companies or stiff competition, they can still easily win with what we offer.

In this section, I introduce them to what we call an Evergreen Website. This website can be cloned hundreds and hundreds of times, moved to any city anywhere in the World, and rank in every area the business wants to work.

I share a brief story about this, but I do not share the entire strategy. I explain that there is too much to show in this short presentation and move on to explain how it will help them scale their business tremendously, even if they alone are competing against big teams of SEOs and Web Designers.

This last nudge is usually the final push they need to get them over the line and have them chomping at the bit to become a client.

They have seen how what I am teaching works, I have shown them how they can do it themselves, and I have also demonstrated how alone they can still take on big teams of SEOs and Website specialists.

Pair this with an irresistible offer at the end, and you

have a high converting sales webinar.

Let's look at the close and how easy it is to create an offer the right ordinance will not walk away from.

THE CLOSE

When done correctly, this will increase sales on your webinars by multiples of ten.

The idea of a webinar is to sell something at the end, usually at a much higher price than on your website but with added bonuses for buying on the Webinar that makes it an irresistible deal. I try to make the value 10 to 1, so if the value is $10,000, then the price will be $1000.

This offer is something the right audience will find almost impossible to walk away from. The whole point is that you are creating an irresistible offer for the right audience.

By this point in the presentation, you should have sold them on your concept, sold them on your beliefs, and sold them on your product. The only problem left is they can go to your website whenever they want and purchase your product.

Because they can purchase your product whenever they feel like it, there is no urgency for them to buy it right now live on this presentation.

We must create this urgency by presenting them with an irresistible offer they find just too good to walk away from.

I do not like to reduce the price; otherwise, all your existing customers who see this offer will want to move over, which can become troublesome. Trust me. I have fallen foul of this several times in the past.

I have also found that those who pay too little for a product do not value it and therefore do not use it and end up requesting a refund or canceling their subscription after a brief period.

I prefer to keep the price similar or higher to the options available on the website and then increase the overall value they receive for buying on the Webinar.

Not only do I increase the scope of the product they get, but I also provide bonuses for buying on live that are not available if the product is purchased directly from the website.

There is a strategy to this, and it is this strategy that makes the offer irresistible to the right audience.

Let's pretend we are selling a piece of software on a webinar that will be used on a website to generate increased revenue.

If the prospect came to your website and purchased the software, they would also need websites to use the software on, hosting for the websites, and they would need to go through all the training on how to use that piece of software before they could generate an income with it.

If you have the right people on the Webinar, and

they need what you are selling, in some cases, the required commitment might still be too much, and they would put off the purchase.

Therefore, we create an irresistible offer that they just cannot walk away from.

If I were selling this piece of software on a webinar, then I would create and offer something like this:

The offer:

- The Software (instead of a one site license, a ten-site license)
- Hosting for ten websites
- Ten pre-designed website templates
- The complete premium training course
- Access to live training from my team and me for the next three months

Looking at the offer like this, we provide everything they need. Still, they may not realize this is everything they need from just looking at the offer, so we also need to plan the delivery to make sure they understand the value of what they are getting and how it all fits together.

At the end of section three, we start explaining how we cannot teach them everything they need to know in a short presentation.

We then explain how we have put together a special offer for those who want to move forward with what we have taught during this presentation, which is only available for them on this Webinar and is the best deal we have ever done (and it should be).

Then we ask them if they would like to see the offer, and we wait for them to confirm that they do. This is another micro-commitment just before the close.

When enough prospects have said yes in the chatbot, we then move onto the close.

We start by saying:

This is what you are going to get today.

The software but instead of a single website license, we are giving you a ten-website license.

A single website license would normally cost you $97 a month on our website.

Today you are getting a ten-website license worth $970 a month.

This is what our existing customer have to say about this (share a couple of reviews or testimonials)

Plus, to make sure you have no additional costs involved, we are also going to give you ten website hosting.

This means you can get rid of your current hosting.

Again, share something nice someone has said about your hosting.

Then we repeat

So, you are getting.

A ten-website license of our software worth $970 a month

Ten website hosting worth $97 a month

And to make sure you have absolutely everything you need, we are also going to include.

Ten pre-designed website templates, so all your website is completely unique.

These would cost you $97 each to buy from (website that sells templates)

That is a $970 gift.

This is what a customer said about our templates (share some more proof)

So, you are getting.

A ten-website license of our software worth $970 a month

Ten website hosting worth $97 a month

Ten pre-designed website templates worth $970

So far, that is a value of $1067 a month plus a gift worth $970.

But I will not stop there because what is the use in having everything you need if you are not completely sure of how to use it?

That is why I am also going to give you access to our premium training course that we usually sell for $970 right here (share the sale URL) completely free of charge.

This covers:

List briefly what each section of the training

covers in a few seconds each and how it will benefit them, then share some more testimonials or reviews of people saying nice things about the training.

Then say. So today, you are getting:

A ten-website license of our software worth $970 a month

Ten website hosting worth $97 a month

Ten pre-designed website templates worth $970

Our premium training course worth $970

So far, that is a value of $1067 a month plus a gift worth $1940.

Now you have everything you need to succeed with this, but I want to make sure every person on here today is guaranteed to succeed with this, which is why I have one more special gift for you.

I am also going to give you full access to me and my team for live training for the next three months this would usually cost you $397 a month on its own.

Then say so today you are getting:

A ten-website license of our software worth $970 a month

Ten website hosting worth $97 a month

Ten pre-designed website templates worth $970

Our premium training course worth $970

And live access to me and my team for the next three months' worth $397 a month

That is a total value of $1464 a month plus a gift worth $1940.

And it would be an absolute bargain at that price.

But I am not going to charge you that today.

I could easily charge you $997 a month for this, and you would bite my hand off.

But today, I am going to shock you because you can get the best possible deal you are ever going to get.

Today it is just.

$147 a month or $997 a year if you commit to taking this for 12 months.

Also, to make sure there really is no risk to you, we provide a full 30 day no questions asked money-back guarantee.

This is an example of an irresistible offer that will increase sales massively for your business. Obviously, the prices and sections are made up for this book, but this is precisely how you piece together an offer for your Webinar.

You will find if you just list the items, sales will decrease massively. What you want to do is:

- List each item in turn.
- Share its value or perceived value.
- Explain how they should use it.

- Share some social proof about it.
- Then list all items included so far and their total value.
- Do this for every item in your offer until you reach the last one.
- Then restate the whole list and its total value.
- Then confirm it would be an absolute bargain at that price, but you will not charge that.
- Then drop the price gradually, stating how it would be a bargain at that price.
- Until you eventually release the ridiculous price for this irresistible offer

Try to give them ten times the value they would get buying each product on the list individually, and your sales skyrocket.

Once the offer is on the table, you want to run through the list of what is included again with a brief explanation of why they need each item so much and how it will help them.

Once you have completed this, transition into the Questions section of the presentation.

THE QUESTIONS

Sometimes there will be questions that you cannot answer during the Webinar, and not answering these questions can result in reduced sales.

To counter this, I like to go through the presentation with as many people as possible before letting a live audience see the Webinar.

I ask whoever I go through the Webinar with to write down as many questions as possible during the presentation and then cross them out when they get answered.

Whatever questions are left in their list at the end need answering.

I then get into the customer's mindset and create as many objections as possible.

If the questions can be answered easily by tweaking the content a little but not affecting the flow and the message, I do that.

After this, I create pre-written questions covering all the remaining objections and carefully craft my responses.

When I move into the questions section, I say I have

time for a few questions live.

I then read the questions I have pre-written and answer them strategically to increase sales.

I then say, right, we have just 5 minutes left, so I am going to share a quick 5-minute countdown video. I will try to answer all your questions in the chat before the timer runs out.

Please add 3 question marks before each question so I can spot them because we have hundreds of people on.

If I miss your question, do not panic. You can still get this fantastic deal today, and my team will help you at support@mysupporturl.com.

Then share the 5-minute countdown video and watch the sales continue to pour in for the next 5 minutes.

FILL IN THE GAPS.

It would help if you used this section to fill in the headlines and reminders for each section of your Webinar before writing it out entirely with whatever presentation software you are using.

If you do not want to ruin your book or use a Kindle, then a PDF of this can be downloaded from https://mikejmartin.com/webinar-resources.

WEBINAR TITLE

How to (the thing they want) without (the thing they hate)

Short Title

How to ______________________________

without______________________________

Longer Title

How to

____

____

Without

____

____

THE INTRODUCTION

Briefly Welcome everyone to the Webinar and ask some personal questions (where they are from, what they do, are they excited) to get them to interact.

Tell them what you are going to cover in today's training.

Hook them to the end by promising those who remain on until the end something special.

Why should they listen to you (achievements or what makes you great)?

What you have done for others (other achievements through you or client success)

What their future will look like after this (something they want but until now have failed to achieve)

The challenges they will face (what is hard about what your teaching)

What they should expect from the presentation (who this is for and what you will cover)

Restate what you are going to cover today (for those who turned up late)

Restate your hook that will keep people on until the end (for those who turned up late)

To transition into the Content section of the presentation, I like to say something simple.

"Let's get started."

THE CONTENT

Break the content into three sections and try to create stories for each one.

Use this story structure:

- I wanted to achieve this.
- I tried by doing this.
- I failed.
- I thought all hope was lost until I discovered this.
- I changed how I did it and started doing it like this.
- I achieved this.

Section one - prove what you are offering works.

Section Title

How to

____

____

Without

Story

I wanted to achieve this.

I tried by doing this.

I failed.

I thought all hope was gone until I discovered this.

I changed how I did it and started doing it like this.

I achieved this.

____
______

____
______

Social Proof

____
______

____
______

Section two - prove that they have the ability to do this.

Section Title
How to

Without

Story

I wanted to achieve this.

I tried by doing this.

I failed.

I thought all hope was gone until I discovered this.

I changed how I did it and started doing it like this.

I achieved this.

Social Proof

Section three - prove that there are no outside forces that can stop them.

Section Title

How to

Without

Story

I wanted to achieve this.

I tried by doing this.

I failed.

I thought all hope was gone until I discovered this.

I changed how I did it and started doing it like this.

I achieved success.

Social Proof

THE CLOSE

Create an irresistible offer.

You need to look at the core item you are selling and find other things they will need to achieve success and include as many of them as possible in the offer.

Item 1

____

____

Item 2

____

____

Item 3

____

____

Item 4

____

____

Item 5

Item 6

Total Value

THE QUESTIONS

Do not do all the questions yourself. It would be best to take others who understand what your customer does through the presentation and see what questions they have.

You may think the questions are silly, or the answers are obvious because they are to you, but they may not be obvious to the audience and therefore need answering.

Question

____

____

Answer

____

____

Question

____

____

Answer

Question

Answer

Question

Answer

Question

Answer

Question

Answer

Question

Answer

Question

Answer

Question

Answer

Question

Answer

Question

Answer

____

____

Question

____

____

Answer

____

____

THE FINAL CHAPTER

By now, you should have most of your Webinar put together and be about ready to start recording it.

Before moving forward and recording your Webinar, go back through the Expert Tips for Your Webinar section of this book and make sure you have included as many of the tips as possible into your presentation as they will increase sales.

The tools I like to use for my webinars are:

- PowerPoint or Google Slides (for creating & presenting)
- GotoWebinar (for live webinars & like live)
- Ever Webinar (for recorded evergreen webinars)
- Camtasia (for recording webinars)

You do not need anything else to create webinars. It is a ridiculously cheap way of promoting your business.

The best ways to market your Webinar are as follows:

- Email Marketing

- Paid Ads
- Affiliates
- Social Media
- Podcast Interviews

If you are interested in reciprocal webinars or would like to practice, then you can promote our high converting $20+ EPC automated webinars by signing up here. https://mikejmartin.com/webinars and I will pay 50% commission for any sales you make and a recurring monthly or annual amount for every sale you make.

For those who sign up more than 50 clients for either of our software businesses, I will review your Webinar for you then have a two-hour one-on-one skype call with you to help you get the most out of your Webinar and increase your chance of success.

You can find third parties with awesome webinars on this page if you're interested in having them run your webinar in exchange for you running theirs https://www.mikejmartin.com/webinar-recips/

I wish you all the luck in the World with your webinar adventure and hope it brings you all the riches and success you deserve.

Thank you very much for reading the first copy of my book. Please come back regularly as the book will be updated each year with new strategies that are working right now.

Please leave an honest review of what you thought.

All the best

Mike Martin

Printed in Great Britain
by Amazon

14028732R00066